Money's Not a Math Problem

The Real Reason You're Broke, And What to Do About It

JADE WARSHAW

RAMSEY
PRESS

© 2024 Lampo Licensing, LLC

Published by Ramsey Press, The Lampo Group, LLC
Franklin, Tennessee 37064

This publication is designed to provide accurate and authoritative information with regard to the subject matter covered. It is sold with the understanding that the publisher is not engaged in rendering financial, accounting, or other professional advice. If financial advice or other expert assistance is required, the services of a competent professional should be sought.

Unless otherwise indicated, Scripture quotations are from THE HOLY BIBLE, NEW INTERNATIONAL VERSION®, NIV® Copyright © 1973, 1978, 1984, 2011 by Biblica, Inc.® Used by permission. All rights reserved worldwide.

Scripture quotations marked MSG are taken from *THE MESSAGE*, copyright © 1993, 2002, 2018 by Eugene H. Peterson. Used by permission of NavPress. All rights reserved. Represented by Tyndale House Publishers, Inc.

Editor: Kris Bearss
Cover Design: Weylon Smith, Chris Carrico
Photography: Seth Farmer
Interior Design: PerfecType, Nashville, TN

ISBN: 978-1942121770

Printed in the United States of America
24 25 26 27 28 JST 5 4 3 2 1

Money's Not a Math Problem

The thief's purpose is to steal and kill and destroy.
My purpose is to give them a rich and satisfying life.
John 10:10
New Living Translation

Contents

Luck of the Draw

I was standing in line at the Publix grocery store on Coral Ridge and Southgate. My husband, Sam, and I used to call it the "old-people Publix," because the area of South Florida we lived in was home to many retirees and snowbirds from New York. Each year they would migrate to South Florida for the winter to escape the northern cold.

So naturally, a much older gentleman was in front of me (in his early eighties, I guessed). I watched him finish his purchase with the cashier, take his bags, and slowly leave the line. Now it was my turn. My stomach tightened. *Here we go*, I said to myself.

The cashier began to scan my groceries. It wasn't much—just a few food staples and a couple other necessities, including a four-pack of Angel Soft bathroom tissue. I knew I couldn't spend much, but bathroom tissue wasn't an option. Before coming to the store, I had done some quick meal planning to determine exactly what we needed to get us to our next paycheck. Now I just needed a little luck. I'd done this dance before, but I knew the rules weren't exactly set in stone.

Sam and I had just under $8 in our bank account. The groceries on the belt would be about $45, assuming I'd calculated correctly. I knew going in that when I scanned my card to pay, I would be overdrawn . . . IF the card went through. But my biggest worry was whether the bank would even allow the purchase without declining my card. I would handle the overdraw later. We needed food now.

I had enough experience with this kind of situation to know that if my balance was negative, it was no dice. But as long as there was a little money in the account, the bank would usually let one purchase slide. And yeah, we'd get hit with the overdraft, but at least we'd have groceries. The key was that the amount over the balance couldn't be too high. Otherwise, it would decline, and I would've missed my shot.

I wasn't sure what the rule was. Was there a rule? If I had $7.83 in my account, would they let a $44.38 purchase through? My mind was working overtime trying to crunch numbers without an actual equation. And my armpits were starting to sweat.

I should've brought a check, I thought. Those usually didn't clear over the weekend, and the funds weren't verified in the moment. So I'd have Saturday and Sunday to get some money in the account before the check cleared. But people didn't really write checks for groceries anymore, so that could look suspicious. *Although this is old-people Publix. Maybe I could get away with it?* I thought.

Before I knew it, my groceries were scanned and I was sliding my debit card through the card reader. I held my breath . . .

Approved.

Oh, thank you, Lord! I exhaled. I smiled at the cashier. "Thanks! Have a great weekend!" I said, as if everything was totally fine.

I'm fine. We're fine. Everything is fine. Everything is fine and dandy and okay.

As if I wasn't just dangling from the cliffs in my own mind, I walked to the parking lot. I needed to get dinner started. Getting into my car, I couldn't help but think about the Publix slogan: "Where shopping is a pleasure." *Huh*, I thought, *not for me. That was agony.*

At the same time, all of this was normal. Paycheck to paycheck. This was my life. This was our life. Would this still be my life when I'm in my mid-eighties? Still shopping at old-people Publix? Still broke as a joke?

It wasn't sustainable. It wasn't healthy. It wasn't good. And there wasn't peace. I knew that, and my husband knew that.

Just because something is normal doesn't mean it has to continue to be, right? Debt is normal. Not having a plan for your money is normal. Floating a lifestyle with credit cards is outrageously normal. Running out of money before the next paycheck hits. Normal. While still pretending to have enough money. Exceedingly normal.

Hiding the truth. Overwhelmingly normal.

Wow. Normal sucks.

Let's change that. And I mean for real this time.

We Don't Need Another Hero

Fact. You don't need another person telling you to budget. You don't need another person telling you to spend less and "live below your means." And you certainly don't need someone to tell you it would be better if you earned more income. If you've done even the most basic internet search on handling money, or you've followed the latest finfluencer on Instagram in an attempt to get your financial act together, you likely have heard this advice and more. But it wasn't enough to change you.

Much like overdrawing your bank account is a symptom of a bigger issue—typically debt, not enough income, spending problems, or a combination of all three—I believe that not being able to do the basic things to solve your situation (like sticking to a budget or plan for your money) is a symptom of a bigger issue. And that issue tends to show its face in the form of doubtful beliefs, fear, and/or flat-out lies.

So this book is not going to be like the other books you've read about money.

It's not a book about numbers, percentages, or decimals. We won't talk about a bunch of stats, and certainly no charts or numerical equations. And I promise you, we won't be doing any math. (I actually hate math and made Cs in those classes my entire academic life.) But what we *will* do is dig deep to identify your fears surrounding money. *What do you believe about money, and where did those beliefs come from?* Next, we will get into the nitty-gritty, calling out those beliefs and seeing if they can stand up to the heat. If not, we will dig them up by the root and replace them with truth and tactics that will finally allow you to carry out a fruitful financial-plan-of-action in your life.

My greatest hope is that you will find hope. My prayer is that this book will help you stop burying your head in the sand.

You will no longer log into your bank account with a pit in your stomach.

You will no longer hide your purchases from others.

You will no longer avoid conversations about money with your spouse.

You will no longer fear growing old with no money and no savings.

You will stop negatively controlling the money in your home and lording it over your family.

You will stop snapping at your kids when they ask for basic needs.

You will stop living paycheck to paycheck.

You will stop padding your purchases with credit cards.

You will stop viewing yourself as a victim and therefor an exception to the rules.

You will no longer be swayed by how your friends and family view your success and failures with money.

You will no longer feel guilt and shame about getting ahead.

I hope you will see that money is totally amoral and completely neutral. It's color blind. It doesn't have a past, and it doesn't have a bias against you. Money doesn't control you; you control it. The only power money has is to make you more of what you already are.

In this book, you will discover and decide who you are going to be with your money.

I want to help you learn the truth that you have the ability to control your finances. A budget can be a powerful tool that you learn to love, not loathe.

Imagine a life where all the bills are paid on time each month. There's even money left over to do the fun things you've planned, like enjoying that trip to the beach or taking your kids back-to-school shopping. Your stress level about day-to-day emergencies is almost nonexistent because you have plenty of money in savings. And instead of fighting about money, you and your spouse have learned to have conversations about it, and each person's opinion is valued.

Yeah, a friend or family member occasionally makes a comment about how "you're really something now," or asks if you're still on your "little budget," but it doesn't bother you like it used to. It rolls off, and you go about your day with confidence.

You go to the grocery store, and instead of worrying about over-drawing your account or being unable to get what you need, you bring an envelope of cash with you, and it has enough in it for you to get the items you've decided on.

Each time you log into your online budget, you get excited because not only can you see all the progress you've made, but you can also see exactly where you're going. And you are on track with your goals.

You have become a person who is confident in managing their money, not fearful of it. Your money mind is right.

You are now the hero in your story. Not a tool, not a plan—you.

Instead of a spark that flickers and flakes out when the slightest wind blows, you have become a voracious financial fire, baby! Wind is your fuel, not your foe, and it only makes you more fierce and more powerful.

It's time to get into it. As my buddy Chris Campbell says, "No more 'one day.' Today is DAY ONE."

This book should be a conversation, not me just yakking at you. I've included questions after each section. Don't blow them off. Take time and sit with them. Evaluate yourself and answer truthfully. Go as deep as you can go with your answers. I might say something you don't agree with. Okay, yell back at me, throw the book across the room if you need to . . . but then keep reading. Remember, we're on the same team.

CHAPTER 1

Hey, Now, You're an All-Star

I'll say it again. We are on the same team.

Just think of me as the team's captain. And if we are getting into particulars, I'd prefer Jordan, not LeBron. I'm just saying I plan on helping us actually win championships regardless of who my teammates are. And not just win. I wanna dunk on whatever dysfunctional beliefs have kept you from getting your money right thus far. I don't need a roster of all-stars. I just need folks who want it. Folks who are interested in getting better at learning to play their game.

But here is the truth: Skills only take you so far. They are only part of the equation. You also have to understand the rules of the game—you can't make it up as you go and hope there won't be any whistles blown. Above all, your mind has to be right. You have to believe you deserve to win just as much as the other guy. You have to believe you have the ability to overcome whatever challenges you face each season and win. As a matter of fact, I'd argue that what you believe is the most important part.

With managing money, you can have all the head knowledge, all the software, and even learn all the lingo. But if you've been lied to or confused about the way the game is truly supposed to be played, you're setting yourself up to lose. And most importantly, if your mind isn't right—if you don't believe you're capable of rising to the financial challenges you face in each season and win with your money— you're sunk.

Now, I am the type of team captain who will get all up in your stuff and hold you accountable so we can win this thing. Some folks don't like that, so if that's you, this may not be the book for you. In that case, we're still cool. Go on and shoot your shot.

But trust and believe when I say I have earned the right to get all up in your stuff when it comes to money and budgeting. I have lost, I have air-balled, and I have played with injuries and disadvantages. I have failed and lost many seasons. But I have also figured out how to come back stronger and tougher mentally, and work my freaking tail off to win the championship and keep winning year after year.

That's what you're about to do too. Jump ball, baby!

The Way We Were

My husband and I got married back in 2007, literally one week after college graduation. Stressful, I know.

And very shortly into our wedded bliss, we realized we were just two broke lovebirds. We both had music degrees and musical aspirations, but we had no money and no real careers. What we had not yet realized is that, combined, we were on our way to racking up

$460,000 of debt, the vast majority of it consumer debt and student loans.

Now it just so happened that someone bought us a Carnival Cruise for our honeymoon. You know, those giant, fun hotels-at-sea that sail you to the vacation destinations of your dreams. The cruise was great, but more than that, it gave us the first clue to solving our money and musical-career dilemmas. Onboard the ship was tons of entertainment. Sam and I knew then and there that THIS is what we wanted to do. So we went home, planned a course of action, and a year later, we were working on a cruise line together as entertainers in one of the onboard variety shows. We were making about $40,000 a year combined, which was far better than the $30K we'd started at, so in my mind, *we'd made it*! (I know, low bar. I'll get to that later.)

Or had we? During this time, we began to notice something that looked a lot like a hot mess brewing just beneath the surface. It was our debt, and it only seemed to be getting bigger and steamier, with more zeros at the end. But Sam and I weren't talking much about it, let alone doing much about it.

The student loan payments (with interest) had started piling up, and our credit card balances were growing with interest and late-payment fees attached. I couldn't seem to understand it . . . Or maybe I just didn't want to. Plus, there were our cars—two of them—one even more expensive than the other.

Yep, the signs that we had a major money crisis on our hands were beginning to show. And it wasn't just us. It was 2008, the Great Recession, and the world had gone mad. Gas was skyrocketing, mortgages were being foreclosed on left and right, and people's fake financial worlds were coming to an end. So we did what any average American does: We tried to hide from it. We basically glossed over it, hoping no one else would notice the ruin either.

Sam and I prioritized our townhome and our expensive cars.

We put our student loans on forbearance. *There, got that out of the way.*

We paid the minimum on our credit cards—well, some of them.

And we paid off a few little $100 ankle biters to feel like we'd done *something*.

And since we worked at sea, without cell-phone service, it was relatively easy (not to mention, convenient) to block out all the debt collectors calling to complain that we were late or behind on our payments.

We even told ourselves we were "working the Dave Ramsey plan," when in reality it was the plan . . . ish. You know, that famous (or infamous, depending on who you talk to) plan where you work through 7 financial Baby Steps that ultimately lead to getting out of debt, saving money, and building wealth *theoretically*. In my head at least, it was still a theory, so it was fine if we tinkered with the plan ever so slightly to make it conform better to our behavior and beliefs.

We can't save $1,000 right now for a starter emergency fund, so we'll just leave that one for later.

Oh, and the plan says to cut up all the credit cards, but we need ours because of the nature of our work.

And then finally, the budget. *Ew.* Vile word. *Okay, so we barely have money to do what we want as it is. Now isn't the time to let a budget take away even more of our money. Not yet anyway.*

Sam and I basically created our own MacGyver-rigged plan based on our beliefs about our money.

Great! Pseudo-solved that one! Consider it successfully swept under the rug. As long as we keep the problem from showing, we Gucci! It doesn't exist.

But the truth remained. The problem did exist. Our MacGyver efforts to accomplish anything monetarily were only moving us at a snail's pace. And the frustration was real. No matter how hard we tried to act like life wasn't lifing the mess out of us, it was.

Inevitably, the time came to deal with it. For us, it was knowing that although our student loans were in forbearance, a day was coming when we would have to pay the piper, and this particular piper had the ability to make our life very difficult. We realized that in order to pay off this debt, we were not only going to have to get serious about a plan for our money, but we would need to embrace a tool that strikes fear in the hearts of many: the dreaded budget.

First, though, before Sam and I could confront the problem (for real this time) and take real actions to solve it, each of us needed to ask, and answer, some very real questions. Deep, personal, like back-in-the-day, childhood kinds of questions.

How in the world did I get here?

Is it possible that I am truly this irresponsible?

Why, really, am I behaving this way?

What am I so freaking scared of?

Why do I think the way I think?

Why do I believe the things I believe about money?

Why am I convinced all the "good stuff" is only for "those people"?

Why have I buried my head in the sand?

I've tried before to manage my money. Why hasn't it worked?

Basically, to echo the infamous words of *The Office*'s Michael Scott, "Why are you the way you are?"

It was clear I would need to commit to a mindset journey, not just a money journey. Sam too. He would have to master his own dragons as well.

But the practical work and the thought work were more than worth it. By committing to both journeys—money *and* mindset—he and I were able to successfully pay off $460,052 of debt in seven-and-a-half years. From there we went on to purchase cars in cash, stack up plenty of emergency savings, and, through our home, our business, and our investments, build a million-dollar net worth.

All things are indeed possible with the right plan and the right mindset.

This Is Me

Now if you're anything like I was, nothing will put a pit in your stomach faster than the mention of the word *BUDGET*. For me, the idea of a "good budget" was almost an oxymoron. I've heard Dave Ramsey say before that the two words *financial peace* don't typically go together, much like the words *airline service* don't typically go together. Well, when I first started out, I felt the same way about the words *good* and *budget*.

In my mind back then, budgets were not good, not necessary, and not effective *for me*. Budgeting had gotten an extremely bad rap because of what I'd seen growing up and what I'd gleaned from uninformed people around me.

A budget was something to be avoided, not embraced. Budgets only caused headaches and arguments—not to mention those jokers are impossible to stick to. Budgets kept you from having new clothes, having fun, and getting to see the world. A budget was a little prison safe that held all the goods, yet no one seemed to have the combination for the lock. The budget never spoke rationally. It only yelled and screamed at you. It only made you feel guilt or shame for "not remembering," "not planning ahead," or "not asking earlier." The budget kept a tight list of priorities . . . and yours were definitely not on it. The budget was a bully in the schoolyard, best to be avoided at all costs. Quite literally.

I had built up a wall of negative belief keeping me in the dark. It was keeping me from seeing over it to the truth on the other side. I'd heard the information and I knew the stats. It wasn't enough. If I was going to make the changes in my money that were so desperately needed, the wall had to come down. And yours does too. One brick of bogus belief at a time, it's time to deconstruct the wall of wrongful beliefs and flat-out lies that keep you from getting to the place of peace that you so desperately want and need with your money.

In order to do this, I'm going to share five lies I previously believed that kept me from winning with money. I will also share five truths that shed light on those lies for what they were and gave me a firm foundation for building a new relationship with money and budgeting. My hope is that these truths will begin to change your beliefs about budgeting and give you practical ways to move forward by implementing them.

CHAPTER 2

Tell Me Lies, Tell Me Sweet Little Lies

Confession. There was a time when I believed the Keebler elves were real. I saw the commercials on TV, and it seemed plausible to me that these little guys had an actual cookie factory in the trunk of a large tree. After all, how else did the cookies end up in the stores? And if not baked with care by magical elves, how else did they taste so damn delicious?

However ridiculous, I believed the elves existed, so I set out on a tree-trunk-inspecting mission to find them. But I could never locate those guys. To my shock and disappointment, the Keebler elves were indeed a lie. No matter how much I wanted to believe it, no matter how much I wanted a secret society of tree elves to be the makers of those cookies, it simply wasn't true, and I wasn't right. And if I wanted to mature and move on, I had to embrace the truth, even as a six-year-old kid.

Time and time again, I have found that my behavior with money is mostly tied to what I believe is true about my money and myself.

And back then, what I believed about money was usually based on an experience from culture, media, or my own life that not only seemed true but often seemed the only logical explanation. And sometimes it even went a step further: I wanted it to be true, because if it was, I got to be right.

In my experience, getting to the bottom of my belief has meant looking to my past and taking the time to drill down and ask myself tough questions. Not only what do I believe, but where exactly did that belief come from? And . . . is it actually true? Many times, to my shock and disappointment, I have discovered that—just like the cookies—if I look around hard enough, I find that what I believed was a lie. It simply wasn't true, and I wasn't right. And if I wanted to mature and move on, I had to accept and embrace the truth, especially as an adult.

So let's do it. Let's start to drill down on the ingrained lies. The lies we believe consciously, or even absent-mindedly, every day regarding our ability to manage our money or, in most cases, a lack thereof.

I will only share my own experience in this book, not lofty ideas or untested theories. I will tell you what worked, what didn't work, what was easy, and what was way harder than I thought it would be. To start, I'm going to share five very true-to-me lies I believed about budgeting and how, as a result, those lies kept me from embracing common sense and the truth about budgeting earlier on in my life.

While I hate to play the *shoulda coulda woulda* game, I can't help but think how much better my financial life would have been if I had recognized and dropped my shoddy money mindset a lot sooner.

Sometimes I think, *Maybe if I had suggested the idea of having a good budget before Sam and I were even married, we would've had a better handle on our income and debt, avoided more debt through credit cards, and been out of debt sooner.* Ah well, hindsight is always 20/20, right? My hope is that by sharing my own mental stumbling blocks, you will see yourself in my way of thinking, or possibly it will prompt you to see some of your own "stinking thinking" (as Joyce Meyer would say) that has to change.

As my longtime pastor and good friend David Hughes says, "It's time to think about what you think about."

LIE #1: Budgets are a form of punishment that restrict you from spending.

One of the clearest money memories I have as a young kid is helping my dad while he organized and paid the bills. Now I was a child of the late '80s and early '90s, so bear with me. Long, long ago, before computers lived in our pockets, my dad had a big gray metal file cabinet in his office, and inside the cabinet were brown file folders. Each folder had the name of an expense category hand-written on a white label, in my dad's signature handwriting—*House*, *Utilities*, *Insurance*, etc.—and inside those folders was where he kept all the statements and check stubs from prior payments.

On Saturdays I would sit with my dad and "help him" pay the bills. Which was basically him asking me to find a folder, and me handing it to him and then putting it back in the file cabinet when he was done. I even remember him firing up the old MS-DOS computer and letting me play Oregon Trail in between file-switching.

It was in these Saturday bill-paying sessions that my dad tried to teach me concepts like keeping your bills organized and paid on time, balancing a checkbook (something people used to do when dinosaurs roamed the earth), and yes, the all-important budgeting. I always looked forward to these sessions helping my dad, but over time, this Saturday afternoon activity with him became an activity that, as a kid, I struggled to understand. Why did we do all of this if none of it seemed to work? What was the point?

If we had a budget, why were there still arguments about money? If budgeting helped, why was there still a struggle over what was spent at the grocery store?

If there was a good budget, why was I often without lunch money or supplies I felt I needed for school? And why was war waged over the price of a simple hair appointment?

Sure, I admit that sometimes kids and adults experience the same scenario in completely different ways, but I'm pretty confident that in this case, no one would argue that money caused lots of tension in our home. Which I imagine—nope, I KNOW—is the case in most homes in America. In most families, bringing up the subject of money or a budget doesn't mean we are about to brush each other's hair and sing "Kumbaya."

The truth is, if asked back then, I'd tell you a budget was a sheet of paper that listed all the things you can't do, in bold, with lots of exclamation marks.

I had only seen the budget seemingly hold my family members back from the things they wanted to do—and some of the things we needed to do . . . and it seemed to leave only a trail of hot tempers and frustration in its wake.

From my point of view, a budget was a punishment. It was a constant instigator. It was the whistle signaling a flag on the play; it sent you to your room, crying, to think about your behavior; and it kept an extremely long record of wrongdoing.

The family budget was constantly shaking its finger in our faces and telling us no. It was always telling me as a kid, "You did something wrong, so here's the consequence." To me, the budget was the reason for the arguing. And the budget made a seven-year-old girl think it was partially her fault.

If this rings true for you in any way, shape, or form, it makes sense that you would want to buck against a budget with all your might. It feels controlling, it feels like constraints, it feels like the reason the answer will always be NO. And where's the fun or freedom in that?

I see you.

I *was* you.

Even as an adult.

But then I realized something: Possibly it wasn't the budget. Possibly it was the person behind the budget.

Maybe you too grew up in a home where you felt controlled or punished by money. Or maybe you've been in an adult relationship where your partner has lorded a budget over you in an attempt to intimidate you or keep you in line. Whatever memories trigger you whenever someone like me tells you the benefits of a budget, I want to remind you, *THIS is not that*. That wasn't a budget; that was a person. And you are different. In the wrong hands, a budget can feel like a weapon. In the right hands, it feels like freedom and peace and protection.

Your budget doesn't have to be toxic, and it won't be—because YOU will be in charge of it this time.

Questions

Now is the time for you to do a little thought work.

- *If what I've talked about in this chapter rings true for you in any way whatsoever—if budgeting has ever been, or felt like, a punishment—take a moment to write your own experience.*

- *Now consider what makes your situation different today. And if it isn't different yet, then before you continue reading, think of the steps you could take to change your situation from unhealthy to healthy.*

LIE #2: Budgets are embarrassing. They're for people who "ain't got no money."

When I was a kid, there was a phrase I heard a lot around the house regarding money. The phrase was this: "We ain't got no money." And then there were the various spinoffs—"I ain't got no money for that." "I just ain't got it." Or, "I ain't spendin' no money on that."

Holla if you hear me! And don't leave me hanging.

So many of us have our version of this phrase that we grew up with.

Now here's the thing. My siblings and I didn't grow up poor, but our family certainly was nowhere near wealthy. If I had to guess, we were somewhere in the middle. Both my parents were super hard workers, had good jobs, and were good at their jobs. We tended to live in modest homes in nicer areas, but in my mind, because I always heard this phrase and saw the results of it, it seemed like there was never any money despite this budget thingy.

It's interesting how we connect the dots as kids, because around age seven or so, I also remember disliking going to church. I mean, I truly dreaded it. My greatest hope was that my parents would accidentally oversleep, and instead of going to Sunday school we would go . . . well, basically anywhere else. I felt this way because I had one dress for church, and each time I went to church, the other little girls in Sunday school made fun of the fact that I always wore the same dress. Ridiculous, I know. But as a kid, I was super embarassed and wanted to avoid this situation at all costs.

Somewhere in my kid mind, I did the math:

I'm embarrassed because I only have one dress.
I only have one dress because "we aint got no money."
We ain't got no money because the freaking budget says so.
The budget is what's causing my embarrassment!

Here are the real facts. Our family was like most families. Despite a good income, and cars, and homes, and even nice neighborhoods, most families had NO margin. No extra, no breathing room. Paycheck to paycheck, that's what it was. So we were not the exception, we were the norm! At my young age, I didn't understand that debt and paycheck-to-paycheck living are what cause moms and dads to wig out sometimes when kids ask for things they want or need. It's not the budget that does it.

Parents feeling that financial crunch is why you have one dress that's either too big or too small instead of at least one that fits. It's why you are late turning in that field-trip money or getting those basketball shoes—because you need to wait until the first of the month "when more money comes in."

Now here's the deal, and hear me very clearly on this. Moms and dads get to choose what the spending priorities are. Period. They get to tell kids no, and they get to decide mundane things like whether or not their daughter really needs more than one church dress, or how urgent those extra school supplies are. But the problem with perpetual phrases like "We ain't got no money" is that there is no hope and no future attached.

Language matters when it comes to money.

"We ain't got no money" sounds hopeless and empty.

As you're reading this, I'm not sure which side of the coin you're on. Maybe you were the kid, like me. Or maybe you are the adult with kids who is currently living paycheck to paycheck and you feel attacked right now. Or maybe for you, that daily mantra, "I ain't got no money," is the theme song stuck inside your head and you're sick of it. All I'm saying is that doing a simple "vocab rehab" can go a long way.

It's as simple as changing up your wording from "We ain't got no money" to something with a better future in sight. Like, "Hey, let's plan a way to make it happen," or "I'm not going to spend money on that this month, but we can plan for it next month," or even, "If we can come up with some extra money, we'll make it happen."

My goodness, what a difference such a small word-change can make! It just feels lighter. It feels like there are possibilities. Because there are!

Proverbs 18:21 says, "The tongue has the power of life and death." Another translation of that same proverb says, "Words kill, words give life; they're either poison or fruit—you choose" (MSG). I wholeheartedly believe this to be true. When it comes to money, what we say and how we say it matters. Your wording can take you from embarrassed and believing you are broke and "It will never change". . . to the hope of "This is the situation right now, but with the right actions, it *can* change."

So yet again, we see that the budget wasn't the reason for the embarrassment and frustration in our household. It was the lack of hope and a future attached to it.

Bad word choices are guaranteed to give the budget a bad vibe.

Questions

- *What do you feel budgeting has kept you from, and why?*

- What are some phrases you say around money, or ones you have ringing in your ears, that set you off?

- Why do those phrases set you off?

- If those phrases are negative, how can you switch them to a positive? Even better, what could you do to prove the negative words wrong?

LIE #3: Budgets ruin your financial status. People with budgets are "bad with money or don't earn enough of it."

Look, for this lie, I have no cute, cuddly story or parallel to help me paint a more convincing point. It's just culture, man. It's the feeling on the streets! Having a budget is not only embarrassing, but it's messing with your status. People on budgets are people who don't earn enough or who are bad with the money they do earn. And I, for one, don't want anybody thinking that way about *me*.

You feel it, I feel it. For whatever reason, there is this belief out there that if you don't have the money to just ball out and buy what you want when you want, you've got financial issues. Anybody who can't say yes without end has money problems. If you're someone who puts any guardrails on your spending, if you sometimes decline a friend's invitation to lunch at a restaurant or put a clothing item back on the rack or stick to $200 max each week at the grocery store . . . it must mean you're bad with money or you don't have enough of it—or both. And for that reason, "*Awww*, you have to go on a budget" (in my most irritating, condescending tone). Like it's some sort of social stigma you're relegated to.

Maybe it's TV, maybe it's media, maybe it's credit card culture that has taught us to believe that spending is supposed to be without limit. You should be able to get what you want. Period. *It's "Hot Girl Summer," and I want these folks to see me going all the way outside!* Or you should *at least* be able to spend money on the things that make other people think you have money. Spending is how you prove your status, maintain your status, and manipulate others' view of you financially. A budget would stop you from being able to do this effectively. In fact, it would do the opposite. A budget would *expose you*. People would start to view you as someone who can't handle what little money you do have.

Here's the problem: I truly, truly believed this into adulthood. I tagged the lies I had picked up about budgets and money from childhood, with all the pressures of the microwave money culture we now live in.

- "If you want it, get it. Today."
- "If my girls order two drinks at brunch, I should be able to as well. If they can afford it, I should be able to afford it."
- "If the folks around you have it but you don't have it . . . what will *they* think?"
- "If your kid's friends have it but your kid doesn't have it . . . what will *they* think?"
- "If your neighbor has it but you don't have it . . . what will *they* think? After all, you live in the same neighborhood."

A budget simply gets in the way of keeping up, and it will make people think we are behind.

The dumb stuff Sam and I did in the very early days of our marriage, just trying to fool ourselves and the people around us that we had money, was crazy. The fact that we had student loan debt out the wazoo and couldn't afford our life as it was, didn't stop us from making some ridiculous choices to prove our status.

Trading in a paid-for, perfectly good, albeit very used Jeep Cherokee for a new Hummer with payments(!!!!) just because Hummers were all the rage, is a perfect example of this madness. Why we ever toured and considered buying a $400,000 house when we already had $400,000 of non-mortgage debt is beyond me. I literally can't believe how brainwashed I was by this ridiculous, unrealistic, costly lie.

All I can say is, apparently the word *no* is very unbecoming and points to problems in your finances. It's never just that you can't afford it right now, or that you don't want to buy it right now. The assumption is much worse. *You're just bad with money.* So as my guy Dave Ramsey says, what do we do? We continue to buy things we can't afford with money we don't have, to impress people we don't even know or like!

Okay, get ready to throw this book across the room, because I'm about to put some folks on blast. Some of ya'll have wised up enough to know that all this status-spending BS "could" be a lie. And you've made a budget, just to seem responsible. Still, you would never mention it out loud.

Now you know, though, because you've seen it on paper. Your spending does indeed have limits. But rather than deal with that, you buy dress after dress or suit after suit (or whatever your thing is), to prove that you can. You let credit cards foot the bill. *After all, that's what credit cards are for, right? And it's fine because I get the points.* And you keep letting yourself believe this lie that you have some sort of status to hold up.

About that status . . . Who are you trying to prove it to? Your family? Your coworkers? Your Instagram followers? Yourself? You're trying to convince somebody that you are "good with money and have plenty of it," when in reality all that hoopla you're going through to prove it, only proves the opposite.

Acting like this? You are bad with money. And you probably don't earn enough to support the lifestyle you're propping up. And you actually, truly, desperately need a budget.

I get to say all that because I did all that. I wouldn't call you out if I hadn't been guilty of the exact same things, plus far more than I could ever list in this book. The good news? Clearly, we can change. Clearly, we can clean up our mindset and beliefs and get ourselves together.

If I could do it, so can you.

Questions

- *Have you ever felt embarrassed about budgeting? Reflect on one of those times and write about it. What was behind the embarrassment?*

- *How has the negative stigma around budgeting kept you from budgeting?*

LIE #4: A budget is just a list of your debts. Any money beyond that is "up for grabs," to use however you want.

Have you ever been close to being right about something, but you leave out or misinterpret one part, meaning that in the end you still got it wrong? This sort of thing happens all the time.

Just be a fly on the wall in somebody's car while they're driving with the radio on. Anyone who's ever sung the lyrics "Comma comma comma comma comma chameleon" has been there, singing the WRONG lyrics at the top of their lungs. (FYI, the words are *KARMA chameleon*: "Karma karma karma karma karma chameleon / You come and go / You come and go-o-o-ooooo." Google it.)

Or maybe Hall and Oates is your jam. Mad respect . . . until you do this: "Because your kiss is on my lips." *Oooo*, so close, but so, so wrong. It's "Because your kiss is on my list." It's LIST, fam, I promise you. I would not lead you astray.

And of course, there's the classic "Hold me closer, Tony Danza." As much as I love Tony Danza and lived for *Who's the Boss?* ('80s babies, where y'all at?), the line is "Hold me closer, tiny dancer."

And finally, my all-time favorite because it's closest to my heart: that time in eighth grade when my mom asked if I'd heard the new song by "Chastity's Child." Who you all probably know as Destiny's Child. So, so close. But also, way off.

It's the same with this idea that a budget is simply a list of your debts, or how much you owe from your bills, and from that point on, all your other money—if you have any other money—is up for grabs.

It doesn't really require any plan other than you doing grossly inaccurate mental math at the cash register. *Yep, that feels right.*

If you're feeling like I'm all up in your grill right now, try not to take it too personally. Remember, this is a list of the things I believed at one time or another as well.

What's challenging about this lie is, much like our song lyrics, it's close enough that most people don't really notice the difference. *I have a budget*, you tell yourself, and you really believe it. At the same time, you know it's not really doing much for you, but hey, it's enough that you can check the box under "Financial Tips I've Tried That Didn't Work." And the result is this: All your "extra" money gets heaped together into one clump with no name, no real intent, and certainly no responsibility. Hundreds and even thousands of dollars get piddled away over the course of months, and you really have no clue what you even spent that money on.

I recently saw a statistic along the lines of, more than 70 percent of people don't know what they spent the previous month. Yeah, I'd say that rang true for me back in the day too. I could tell you what my fixed costs were, such as rent or mortgage and cell phone, but if you asked me, "Hey, what did you spend on groceries? What did you spend at Target on crap you didn't need? How much did you spend eating at restaurants or ordering takeout?" I can assure you I did one of three things:

1. I'd brush the whole thing off and act like it's no big deal.
2. I'd lie and make up a "reasonable" number that made me look reasonable.

3. Or I'd genuinely try to make an educated guess and sound confident while being wildly incorrect about the real number, which was unbeknownst to me.

And here's the kicker. If you had asked me, "Do you have a budget?" I would have said yes!

I was close—a budget *does* list your debt and bills. But I later discovered I was still way off. My lyrics needed adjusting.

I didn't realize that including my "extra money" (my discretionary funds) in the budget was part of the song. In my mind, I had done the responsible thing by making sure I was paying my fixed bills that I owed others. But what I was leaving out was any accountability beyond that. I didn't think this other money mattered nearly as much. It's called *discretionary* funds, right? Found money! Extra money! Can't we just blow that? You know, treat yo'self?

Not until later did I realize that the *treat yo'self* mentality was keeping me and my husband from accomplishing anything real. It took learning how much debt we had, and how things needed to change, before we saw just how important our extra money was. I figured out firsthand that knowing your numbers is not just for the folks on *Shark Tank*.

More than that, though, I had to get to the bottom of my deep-down dislike of having accountability in certain financial areas.

Truth be known, I liked the lie. And you probably do too. Because this belief let me do exactly what I wanted to do, which was spend like there was no consequence. But my belief in the lie couldn't help me do what I knew I needed to do, which was get my freaking act together. So I had to dig deep and ask myself why.

I knew why, so the answer came quick. It was because I'd always felt confined and controlled by money. And the solution, as I'd viewed it, was giving myself "ultimate freedom." No limits on my spending. No accountability or plan for my money except making sure my bills were paid. But as I found, there was an irony in that mindset: What I thought was ultimate freedom was keeping me in debt—the complete opposite of financial freedom.

Now it's time to pause and ask yourself these same questions. And you need to be honest.

Questions

- *What is a budget to you? Is it just a list of debts and bills?*

- *Do you think you should be able to spend freely whatever money is left? Why?*

- *Which areas of spending do you dislike having accountability for?*

Finally, dig deep into your memory and come up with why you think that is.

• *Why?*

Okay, now, be honest. Did you kind of like the lie? Sometimes we like the song better the way *we* were singing it, and we'd just rather not change. But we need to if we want to be right.

LIE #5: I should do a separate budget from my spouse. It's better, and I'll have more freedom.

For years, Sam and I have taught a class on money management. The class is called *Financial Peace University*, and we've always been very passionate about teaching it because the content encapsulates the same 7 Baby Steps that helped the two of us pay off almost half-a-million dollars of debt, build up our savings, purchase a home, and invest with confidence. The best part? We did all of it together.

The class runs for several weeks and provides extensive training on all things money, and at the crux of the teaching is, of course, the budget. Among all those classes with all those couples over the years, one theme and one question emerged time and time again: "Do I really have to combine my money and budget with my spouse?" Or the inverse: "I'd like to combine my budget with my spouse, but I just can't seem to get him or her onboard."

Hold on to your butts and gird your loins, because we are about to go there. The gloves are off. This lie is about to hit many of us where it hurts: in our accountability parts.

"I can do a budget on my own. I don't need or want to involve anyone else," says the controlling husband . . . says the wife who likes to do everything her way . . . says the single guy who's good with numbers . . . says your unmarried best friend who spends like crazy despite her "goals."

Truthfully, we like to be in control, right? And why not? We are full-grown adults. You're the sole breadwinner of the family and she *just* stays at home with the kids anyway. Or you're an independent woman who don't need no man. Or better yet, you've worked hard and sacrificed a lot to get to this place financially; you're not about to answer to anyone when it comes to you or your money.

It is easier to have full control of a situation when you see to it that YOU have full control. You set up the fortress so that no one else gets to see inside, no one else gets to interject, no one else gets to raise questions or concerns. When you don't have to share your plans, your course of action, your purchases, or your mistakes with anyone, you get to be the big boss and enjoy the spoils of having no accountability. Consequently, many couples set out to create their own separate budgets, and their own separate plans, with their own separate money. Which amounts to, basically, going their own separate directions in life.

I get why. Money conversations are hard! Each person has an opinion. You think your spouse wants to spend entirely too much, or maybe it's the opposite—he or she is a tightwad who never wants to have any fun. So it's just easier and safer to keep things separate.

There's the all-too-common family dynamic where one spouse—we'll call that person "the beaver"—creates a budget, a plan, and a direction for the entire family's financial life, while the other spouse—who we'll call "the ostrich"—is fine with burying their head in the sand and remaining in the dark. In their own words, they are fine with letting "the responsible one" bear the full brunt of the financial decisions. "After all, she is good with money and good at math, and she makes more than I do. So it's fine if she makes the decisions."

Situations like this only work until there is trouble in paradise. Until either the Beaver starts feeling the heat of doing all the work, or the Ostrich starts feeling the darkness of not knowing or not having a vote.

For some people, though, it's way deeper than that. It's not just that they want control for control's sake. Some folks believe they need this control in order to learn from their past.

I talk to people all the time who have had bad experiences with shared money and budgeting. Divorcees whose ex was a tyrant with the money and tried to cut them out or cheat them financially. Or a spouse who spent like crazy and blew their hard-earned money. I've talked to single moms who at one point depended on their husband's income, but when the marriage fizzled, these women were left high and dry, with hardly a cent to their name. I've talked to people who have been in relationships where there was abuse, or carelessness, or control (or a combination of them all), and the overarching sentiment remains: *When it comes to money, I ain't sharin' nothin' with nobody. I love this person, but when it comes to the loot, he's on his own . . . she's on her own.*

Everyone has their why. Everyone has their reason they believe that budgets are best done alone. And it doesn't just have to be the situations we've faced as adults. As you've read from my own life, so much of what any of us believes is formed by what we experienced as kids. If you witnessed your mom or dad being screamed at for spending too much money, you could easily feel this way about a budget. If you ever had to help your parent sneak around or hide money, a budget could make you feel like this all over again. If you were a kid who had to sacrifice and give your own money to your controlled or abused parent, I know you feel this way.

Man, if that's you, I see you. These are the sorts of situations that affect people to their very core, solidifying the belief that sharing money leaves you at risk and far too vulnerable, and that certain things like budgeting are best done alone.

This fifth lie lures us to believe that by financially closing ourselves off to the people we are supposed to love and trust and depend on the most, we will somehow have, what? More happiness? More closeness? More trust? Surely not more communication! How would that even be possible with a giant barricade of money mistrust surrounding you?

This lie also reinforces the idea that all situations are the same, all people are the same, and all relationships end up the same. It leaves out the fact that marriages don't have to be toxic and that relationships aren't necessarily riddled with reasons for distrust. It leaves out the fact that your current relationship doesn't have to be a mirror image of the worst relationship you've had.

This lie leaves out the freedom, choice, and hope that people can be good, people can be different, and people can change. With the right mindset and the right beliefs, relationships *can* be healthy.

Relationships *can* be restored. Relationships *can* be completely reimagined.

Questions

- *How has a relationship darkened your views on shared money or budgeting?*

- *Imagine a relationship where you could consider sharing money with a spouse. What would that look like?*

CHAPTER 3

Truth Hurts

Digging up your thoughts and beliefs about budgeting and money is not fun or easy. We've allowed these lies and beliefs to freely roam about the cabin of our mind for years, maybe decades. But what we are doing together in this book is such important thought work. In the words of my buddy Dr. John Delony, "we must demand evidence" of our thoughts to hold them accountable. Are they true? Are they productive?

Now that we've laid out the lies on paper, it's easier to see the evidence of how those lies have held us hostage, keeping us stuck in stigma, doubt, and disbelief. It's time to rebuild. Let's make it our mission in this moment to open up our minds and hearts to a better way. Let's recognize that what we believed before was not only counterproductive, but in many cases, it was situational, and in just as many cases, it was flat-out untrue. Those old beliefs kept us locked in the past with a thrown-away key. Until today.

Today, we start the process of embracing a new, proven, and productive set of beliefs . . . beliefs that are actually true.

Now I'm going to walk you through five budgeting truths I have embraced for myself. Not only are these beliefs actually true, but I've decided they will be true for ME in MY life. Because at this point in my life, I refuse to be a victim of old beliefs that have gotten me nowhere.

TRUTH #1: A budget doesn't confine your money. A budget defines your money.

So it turns out I was wrong all that time.

All those years, I thought a budget would only restrict me.

All those years, I thought a budget was a punishment keeping Baby in the corner. (If you don't get this '80s reference, I can't help you anymore.)

But I was flat-out wrong. Not only did I lack the information; I was lacking in technique.

The proper way to construct your budget puts the power in your hands. A good budget should feel like custom organization for your money. YES! I like the sound of this. My girl Rachel Cruze says, "A budget gives you permission to spend." What I'm saying is, we get to choose how we look at things. And having all the details to create context and proper perspective is key!

Having worn glasses since the eighth grade has given me a great appreciation for the details. I wouldn't say I have terrible vision, but there are certain variables that vastly affect how clearly I can see. One of those variables is light. The dimmer the light, the blurrier my vision gets. For this reason, it's imperative that I have my glasses on if I'm going to be driving at dusk or into the night.

Several years back, my husband and I were sitting at a red light as the sun was beginning to set. A car pulled up next to us. I did a double take when I saw who was in the driver's seat. *Was that a goldendoodle? Wearing glasses? Driving? What in the world! How was this possible? Let me pull up IG live.* I was legitimately flummoxed. I squinted with disbelief. Realizing my glasses were in the center cupholder, I hastily grabbed them and slid them over my eyes. Immediately I realized the goldendoodle was a woman with beautiful blond, curly hair and cool hipster frames. *Wow,* I thought, *I was way off.* With my glasses on, I was able to see without limitation and have clear context of what was going on around me.

When it comes to our beliefs about budgeting, some of us have had limited sight and lived somewhat in the dark. We were given a glimpse and formed a false opinion based on what little we could see. I want to help us put on our glasses and shine a bit of light on the topic to not only gain information but hopefully change our perspective.

In the right light, a budget is not a sheet of paper that confines us. It's an organizational tool that defines us.

Like I said before, think of a budget as custom organization with your money. Picture Kim Kardashian's closet. I promise you, all those expensive designer clothes aren't thoughtlessly tossed in a pile in the corner or strewn across the floor. No, it's just the opposite. There are floor-to-ceiling compartments, baby! A shelf for each pair of shoes.

A hook for each purse. Each item has been given incredible attention in detail. A place for everything and everything in its place.

And she has chosen every piece in her closet. Nothing just haphazardly lands in her wardrobe. There is zero madness, only method. Her mindset is: *We aren't simply putting clothes on our back. We are forming an entire look.* With each piece in the closet, anyone who knows her style would say, "Yep, that looks like Kim."

Now that's what I'm talking about! This is the way your budget should function. You work hard, precious hours for your money. That's time away from your family, time away from your friends. You sacrifice sleep, and some of you sacrifice your sanity, to earn your paycheck. What I'm saying is, your money is expensive! Treat it with care. Treat it with intention, not just as stuff heaped in a pile in the corner. It's time to get this money organized.

The same way Kim selects what items are in her closet, you get to select what items are in the budget. And we divvy these items into cash compartments.

Remember the goal here. We are forming an entire look, not just putting clothes on our back for the day. So let's make sure we keep a holistic vision in mind as we curate our cash.

When organizing money, or budgeting, I like to keep three rules in mind.

1) *Be detailed.* This is your chance to choose, so don't leave anything out. If it's part of your life, if it's important to you and your goals, it needs to be in the budget.

Following the same attention to detail as Kim's closet, we need to avoid large heaps of money by detailing line items in our budget. For example, *Food* is not very specific. That's like Kim hanging her leather pants with her jeans . . . Yes, they are all pants. But she would never.

Let's organize this line item further, shall we? I suggest separate compartments for groceries, restaurants/takeout, holiday meals, and even your morning coffee run. This ensures that each item gets the love and funding it deserves rather than getting lost in the shuffle. Be sure to keep this idea in mind when selecting and organizing all your categories.

I should also add that really great closets allow for some empty space should your wardrobe expand. So does a good budget. Make sure you assign an empty line for *Miscellaneous* or *Cushion* in case a new expense you weren't expecting pops up. It doesn't need to be a lot of money. Just a little breathing room should your budget unexpectedly need to expand.

2) *Be realistic.* Listen, Season 29 Kim is *nooottt* keeping clothes in the closet from Season 1 Kim. First off, those jokers don't fit, won't fit. Plus, they are out of style. Trying to wear those pieces would only set her up for failure. That's just being realistic.

The same is true with your budget. You've got to be realistic about the dollar amounts you assign for each category. If you are a "family of 4" trying to squeeze into a "25 and single"-sized grocery budget, you are only setting yourself up to fail. I can't stress how important it is to be realistic and to also accept that seasons change.

Look, gas used to be cheap. Now it's more expensive. We have to acknowledge our reality and simultaneously be willing to adjust for changes. Which leads me to my final organization tip.

3) *Be flexible.* You've finally gotten your money laid out just the way you like it—but wait, what's this? An unexpected item shows up: Your free trial from that streaming app expired and now you're on the hook for $12.99 There's no place for it in the budget closet! You've already assigned every dollar a compartment. Or perhaps you ended up spending more in one area than you planned.

All is not lost. These are the times we have to learn to be flexible. You can pull a little money from a less-important compartment to create space in the budget for that surprise expense. (And I will note, the more detailed you are, the less this will occur.)

There you have it! A beautifully organized budget that reflects your money style. It includes everything from those must-have staple items like rent/mortgage, food, utilities, transportation, and various types of insurance, to seasonal items like birthdays, back-to-school, and holidays—all broken down into detailed compartments with the amount of money of your choosing.

This is what makes budgeting fun and freeing. *You* choose how you will spend each dollar of *your* money. This is also the beauty of a budget that has you in charge. You get to curate it based on your goals. So whether you're working to pay off debt, saving to pay cash for a car, or setting aside funds for a trip to Europe, you decide.

You can choose to lower other category amounts to free up money toward your goals, and you get to set the speed limit. You can be intense and go pedal-to-the-metal by cutting down to bare bones in certain categories, or you can choose to simply be intentional—not necessarily making large, sweeping cuts, but putting whatever extra you have aside without stress or additional sacrifice.

So now we've learned a new truth about budgeting. It doesn't keep you from your money. Instead, it helps you keep up with your money. It doesn't confine your money; it defines your money.

Questions

- *What are some things you need to add to your budget that you've never considered until now?*

- *What is a line item you struggle to keep realistic. Why?*

TRUTH #2: Budgets aren't for people who don't have money. Budgets are for people who refuse to have no money.

The idea (and the embarrassing stigma attached to it) that budgets are only for the poor, or for people who "ain't got no money," is foolishness. As a matter of fact, it's the exact opposite. And I'll tell you why.

Budgets are not the *consequence* for people living paycheck to paycheck. Budgets are the *antidote* for people living paycheck to paycheck. You get me? Proper budgeting is for people who want off the hamster wheel of barely making it till the next check. They want to know there's more purpose to their work than just working to pay bills.

People who budget the right way do so to ensure they are *never* left high and dry. They craft their budget in such a way that their needs *and* goals are satisfied throughout the month. Proper budgeters are not only detailed, realistic, and flexible, but they have mastered the art of paycheck planning.

That's right, there is a right way and a wrong way to budget. So listen carefully.

If you have ever struggled with your budget not working, and wanted to give up, I'd be willing to bet you weren't paycheck planning.

"Oops, ran out of money for the last grocery trip. How'd that happen?"

"Dang it, 1 paid the rent too soon! Now we don't have enough money for gas this week."

"Shoot! I told my daughter I'd get her that dress for Easter Sunday, but it will be too late by the time we get paid again."

This is the frustration many of us have faced when trying to get our money organized. You've followed the advice of being detailed, realistic, and flexible. You can see, based on your income, that you have enough to cover all the expenses listed. So why does it seem there is still a shortage when it's time to make the insurance payment?

One critical step is being left out: You have to decide *when* to spend each dollar and confirm that it works with when you get paid. For each income disbursement, you need to choose which line items will be spent.

This idea of planning your cash flow becomes even more important if your income fluctuates monthly or you don't always get paid on the same schedule. But once you learn to properly plan your paychecks, you won't unexpectedly come up short. You can be prepared, and you can be confident that your bank balance will be where you need it, when you need it.

Where's the embarrassment in that? There isn't any. Quite the opposite. You can take pride in the fact that your money is on point and being managed well with the plan you created.

I would be remiss if I didn't mention one other thought, because there are plenty of people who might say, "But, Jade, I'm doing everything you said and I still feel like 'I ain't got no money'!" This means a couple of factors are being forgotten.

Increase your income. Remember, a budget manages your money; it doesn't make you money. It operates based on what you feed it, and some of you may need to feed your budget more money. Depending on your situation, this could shake out in different ways. On the shallow end of the pool, there are things like side-hustles and picking up extra hours at work. But some of us may need to jump off the deep end and consider long-term core-income increases that could involve new career paths, additional certifications, or moving to an area with less expense and more opportunity.

Live a little. It's also possible you just need to live a little and plan for fun and entertainment and things that give you life. Yeah, it's a drag sending all your money out and never seeing any of it for the things you enjoy. You have control over that. Sure, you need to honor your goals, but even with intense goals, it's important to include reasonable fun or occasional celebration in order to stay motivated and enjoy life.

TRUTH #3: Budgets are like toothbrushes—everyone needs one.

If you've ever watched a soap opera, sitcom, or rom-com featuring two lovebirds in bed, you'll know what I'm talking about. The couple wakes up at the same time from a blissfully restful night's sleep without a hair out of place. Somehow the woman's make-up is still perfect, and the man has no shadow of stubble on his face. Forget any crust in their eyes or crust on their lips, these two lovebirds wake up within millimeters of each other, face to face. Then the woman breathes an airy "Good morning" to the man. Without wincing or gagging, he immediately pulls her close for a kiss. French style, *mmmm mmmm mmmm*, no slime or nastiness there. Only good old-fashioned, realistic love. The stuff movies are made of.

Only problem is, I'm watching the show and I can't help but yell across the room at the TV, "They ain't gonna brush their teeth or *nothing*, Jesus?"

Yeah, right. It's about that time I reach for the remote and click to another show. How about *Dr. Pimple Popper*? It's hard to watch too, but at least it's real.

These types of shows cause us to build up a false standard in our head. We start to believe that: (1) there's something wrong with me if I wake up with funky breath, or (2) we're in a bad relationship, or worse, maybe we don't love each other enough, if I don't want to make out with my spouse first thing in the morning with funky breath. The standard set is so unrealistic that it makes us feel we are the exception rather than the rule.

Allow me to set you free. This is what toothbrushes were made for, and why everyone has one. If you wake up and don't brush your teeth, your breath is what is now known as *ratchet*. Brushing your teeth as soon as you wake up is the rule.

As we saw in the lies about budgeting, so many people have fallen into this same trap regarding what TV, movies, and the media tell us about money. "You should just be able to wake up and spend, baby! Ball out with no budget and no limits! Anyone who checks in with their budget, who checks their account balance first, must have financial issues. And if you can't just walk up and spend, it must mean you're bad with money or you don't earn enough. *Those* are the folks who need budgets."

Nope. Everyone needs a budget, just like everyone needs a toothbrush. Without it, things get ratchet real quick.

I would also add that in the same way brushing your teeth is an important daily hygiene habit, budgeting and money management should be daily financial habits. This idea that you can wake up and spend without planning or boundaries is completely misleading and unrealistic. Making it a habit to log in to your budget each day to see what's available to spend in each category is simply good financial hygiene that everyone should practice.

Why is this important for your money? Think about what happens when somebody consistently skips brushing their teeth. After a while, it's not just a matter of terrible breath. That person also ends up with a case of long-term tooth and gum disease. Your money is the same. You can't outearn bad financial hygiene for long. Pretty soon it will catch up to you in the form of its own kind of disease— debt, stress, lack of savings, or worse.

Regardless of what culture may have us believe, checking in with a plan for your money each day allows you to make sure everything is as it should be. You can verify that your finances are in good health, and you can spend as planned.

Your daily financial hygiene routine should include:

1) *Checking your account balances.* This gives you a quick state-of-affairs. If today is the 29th of the month, funds may be at their lowest. Knowing exactly what you have in the bank can prevent any unplanned or impulsive card swipeage.

2) *Tracking your transactions.* Okay, this is a biggie. If you've ever had an important conversation with someone and later discovered you had spinach stuck in your teeth the whole time, you know the agony of regret. You thought running your tongue along your teeth would do the trick—no mirror needed—but you were wrong. If only you had stopped off in the restroom after you ate to do a quick check . . .

Tracking your transactions helps you avoid the spinach in your teeth. Each day you can look at what was spent and deposited the previous day and start with a clean view of what you can spend today.

When you don't do this, you're assuming you can just run some quick numbers in your head. Later, though, you will have the pain and regret of accidentally overspending in some category. *Spinach, struck right there between your two front teeth.*

3) *Doing a quick check-in with your spouse (if applicable).* Last but not least, have a brief conversation with your spouse each day. It might be something like, "Just a reminder: I'm filling up the car on my way to work," or "Remember the mortgage is coming out today," or "I saw we had a refund come through. Let's talk later about what we want to do with it." Those little check-ins go a long way to keep both of you on the same page.

TRUTH #4: A budget is the map that leads to all your money goals.

It was painful admitting to you that at one point I thought a budget was just a list of all my debts, and I could do whatever I wanted with the amount I had left. Instead of treating that margin like it mattered, I treated it as a free-for-all.

Now I know better.

Being a cohost on one of the top money shows in the world, I learned I was not alone in believing that lie. So many people handle their money this way, only to realize they don't have much to show for it.

For the average American, millions of dollars will pass through our hands over the course of our lifetime. And since I promised I wouldn't make you do math, I'll just run some quick rough numbers. If you work for 40 years from age 25 to age 65 and average $100,000 per year, that's 4 million dollars. *Sheesh!* is all I'm sayin'. To work that long and not be debt-free at the end of it; to not have a paid-for home, and some significant savings, and wealth built . . . that just seems, to be blunt, irresponsible. And to be clear, I was on the fast track to irresponsible, spending my margin on McDonald's instead of what truly mattered for my future.

But here is what I discovered. A budget doesn't just help you pay your monthly mortgage and cell-phone bill on time so you can use the rest to go out on the weekend. A budget can help you strategize for the long-term as well.

As a matter of fact, the truth I want you to embrace today is to view your budget as a financial roadmap that leads to all your money goals. But in order to make a good map, you have to be clear on your destination. Where are you going? And what are your goals?

I'll start. Back in 2009, my husband and I had a clear financial destination in mind: debt freedom. We knew that in order to get there, we'd need to set up our goals correctly and follow the right plan of action to achieve them. To do this, we embraced a plan based on seven major goals. Each goal builds on the previous one. You may have heard of this plan before. It's called the Baby Steps, and it was developed by Dave Ramsey.

The Baby Steps are a tactical, layer-by-layer approach to getting out of debt, saving money, and building wealth over time. All very good goals to have! The plan utilizes a simple format of seven steps.

Baby Step 1: Save up or set aside $1,000 as a starter emergency fund.

Baby Step 2: Temporarily pause investing or retirement contributions and use all additional money (including existing non-retirement savings) to intensely pay off all your debts, except for your home, using the Debt Snowball method.

Baby Step 3: Now stack up 3–6 months of basic living expenses as a fully funded emergency fund.

Baby Step 3b: Save for a down payment for a home purchase. (You can do this in tandem with Baby Step 4 or before moving to Baby Step 4.)

Baby Step 4: Contribute 15 percent of your gross income to retirement investing. (If you aren't also doing Baby Step 3b, you can do the next two steps at the same time as this one if they apply to you.)

Baby Step 5: Start saving the amount of your choice in a 529 or ESA college fund for each of your kids.

Baby Step 6: Pay extra on your home mortgage to pay it off faster. You don't have to be intense about this one, just intentional.

Baby Step 7: You made it!! Now it's all about being generous, continuing to build wealth through additional investing, and enjoying the life of financial peace you've created.

Now this is a quick read. I don't have the space or word count to be able to debunk any lies you may believe surrounding these Baby Steps goals. For now, you just need to trust me that they are not pipe dreams. These are real possibilities, and soon-to-be realities, for people who get on the right kind of budget and plan for their money.

Each day we receive calls on *The Ramsey Show* where people share about which Baby Step they're on and seek strategy and advice to most efficiently get to the next step. Millions of people have called in, visited the lobby, or had their own personal moment declaring "We're debt-free!" or "We paid off our home!" or "I'm a Baby Steps Millionaire!" These are everyday people with everyday salaries who decided to do something meaningful with their margin. And I'm proud to be one of those people.

When you begin focusing on a specific goal, and you have a clear target in mind, you start to ask your budget some important questions: *If I paid a little extra on my car loan, how quickly could I pay it off? I wonder if we start saving for college now, how much we would have by the time our daughter is 18?* The best kind of budget should have no problem answering these questions for you. Not only that, but the best kind of budget should even do the math for you. More on that later.

TRUTH #5: Budgeting requires accountability and trust.

This is the budgeting truth that we all hope to hit the snooze on and continue sleeping, but it's my job to wake you up! And to do so with an aggressively loud alarm.

I spent the early part of my adolescence growing up in northeastern Oregon. We lived in a cornflower blue house at the end of a cul-de-sac. The house was quaint, with three bedrooms all on one level along the same short hallway. Mom and Dad in one bedroom; my sister and me in another; and my only brother at the time had a small room to himself.

I guess since our rooms were situated so close to each other, my parents figured they could make mornings easier by waking us all up at the same time. Without fail, at 6 AM, their alarm would go off. But it wasn't any old beeping or buzzing alarm—it was the "Hallelujah Chorus" from Handel's *Messiah*. If the volume dial only went to level 10, it sounded like somehow my mom and dad found a way to get it to level 20. I often picture that first scene in *Back to the Future*, where Marty McFly goes over to Doc's studio, plugs in his guitar, and turns up that giant speaker as far as it will go. When he strums his guitar, it's so loud, the sound from the speaker completely blows him away.

This was my parents' alarm. Shrieking "Hallelujah" in our faces! And it worked. We would all wake up. Though a bit shell-shocked, everybody in the family knew exactly what to do next. It was time to commence our tightly choreographed routine to get ready for the day.

The alarm I'm setting off today is this: Budgets are best done together with accountably and trust. I'm hoping this is your wake-up call. And though you may feel a bit shell-shocked, don't worry. I'll show you exactly what to do next. My hope is that you and your spouse will be willing to create a tightly choreographed routine to manage your money together, along with a budget that works for both of you each day.

So let's get into it. But first I must say, this fifth truth is not the case for everyone. If your spouse has any sort of addictions that bleed into the money, this particular advice is not for you. In fact, if your spouse has an addiction, it's the opposite: He or she probably needs restricted access to the money. You need to insure that you and your family's finances remain safe, and I would recommend counseling to determine if or when the money should be shared again.

If your spouse is abusive in any way, I'm also waving a red flag. You cannot trust this person. And trust is a key component to sharing money or being in a relationship. Until trust is earned, you need to keep yourself safe, and that includes the money. So many people stay in abusive relationships because they relinquished control of their money to an abusive partner. And now they feel fearful and stuck, unable to leave for lack of money. I hate to see this. I want to prevent this at all costs.

Here is a framework to follow in order to evaluate if you need to keep your money SAFE.

Seek counseling if you experience the following:
Abuse or addiction
Financial infidelity
Evaluate your options and move forward

Treasure

For the rest of us who just want to have our cake and eat it too, I'm going to challenge you. If the idea of sharing your money makes you uneasy, it's time to have some real talk with yourself first, and then to start sharing your heart with your spouse.

I think we all know those cute adages like "Teamwork makes the dream work," and they are true—you will accomplish goals faster by working together and pooling your money. Then there is just that old-fashioned idea of "being one." One united front, with shared goals and full access to each other's lives. There's a verse in the Bible, Matthew 6:21, that says, "Where your treasure is, there your heart will be also." I want to know that my spouse's heart is with me and mine is with him. Sharing our treasure is one of the ways we do that.

A good budget has input, direction, and feedback from both spouses. It's not one dictator in control, or every man for himself. It should be a joint effort, with each line item and amount decided on together. And both of you should have a clear understanding of your budget and agree to why you are spending your money a certain way.

The accountability is built in when both people commit to the budget, and the trust is built further when both spouses prove it by doing their part. Being able to accept being called out when your behavior doesn't align with the budget proves you to be a ride-or-die partner. And getting to know your spouse well enough to know the best way to call him or her out proves you are truly on the same team.

Talk That Talk

I mentioned this idea earlier in another context, but I want to mention it here as well. Language and word choices matter! And when it comes to budgeting, most couples need to do what I refer to as a vocab rehab.

Instead of using terms like "*my* money," "*my* account," "*his* debt," or "*her* bill," incorporate language like, "It's *our* money" and "*We* got paid." As Dave Ramsey says, "When you get married, you become French: we, we."

Just the act of changing around the words you use regarding money can promote unity.

Don't You Forget About Me

Someone is reading this right now and asking, "Jade, what about me? My spouse is not addicted or abusive. They are simply unwilling. Unwilling to budget with me, unwilling to share, and at this point, unwilling to go to counseling to settle it. I have goals, and I'm tired of waiting around for them to get a clue. What about me?"

I'd say, lead by example and always treat your husband or your wife the way you want to be treated. Tell them your goals even if they don't share back. Communicate the payments you're making, the debts you're paying off, the money you're saving, and the traction you are seeing. And continually remind them how much you would love to be working together instead of separately.

This is it. This is what I have found to be true, not just in my own life, but in the lives of countless people who have allowed me to give them financial counsel.

It turns out that money and budgeting don't have to be this negative scheme intended for punishment, embarrassment, or relational power. The right budgets—the best budgets—set people free to accomplish their money goals with control and confidence. So, one last time, let's dig into our thoughts.

Questions

- *If you are married or plan to be married, are you ready to consider the idea of combining money with your spouse? Why or why not?*

- *What things would need to happen in order for you to combine your money with your spouse?*

CHAPTER 4

Sledgehammer

Let's imagine for a moment that you have a home project you know needs addressing. You've put it off for a while, but it can't wait any longer. The good news is, you're willing to get to work to fix it.

You walk up to the workbench and you see a bunch of beautiful tools laid out. From the old tried-and-true, "get 'er done" tools to the new high-tech equipment designed to make the job as easy a 1-2-3, it's all there for you, ready for the taking. But not so fast. There's just one problem. Your hands are tied tightly behind your back.

So what do you do? Well, you have a few choices. You could decide you'll never be able to operate a tool with your hands tied, and immediately give up and walk away. Another choice might be to do the best you can considering the circumstances. You fumble to try and pick up a tool with your teeth, or your toes, or maybe between your chin and your neck—none of which is effective for using the tool properly. Your efforts are so clumsy and unproductive that you finally give up on the whole dang project. Another option is, maybe someone else can come fix things for you. *Unlikely*. Then there is the most logical answer. Let's figure out a way to untie your hands so that you're able to work freely to do the job yourself.

My hope is that over these chapters, I've been able to help you untie and free up your hands to use the tools you need to get your money under control once and for all. Before this, you were frustrated and ready to quit. For far too long, the toxic BS kept your hands bound up behind your back with a zip tie of unbelief. But now you're free. You know the truth: No one is doing it for you—you are the hero.

You did what was necessary to untie those restraints, and you're ready to get to work for real this time. Now it's time to approach that table of tools with confidence. The only challenge you face at this point is which tool to choose.

The Problem with Paper

When Sam and I decided to truly get serious about our money and get on a budget, I started the only way I knew how. On paper.

I'll be honest, it was extremely primitive. On a legal-sized pad of paper I wrote down an estimate of what we might earn that month, and then I listed our normal fixed bills (items like rent, phones, student loans, car notes, insurance—expenses where the amount was the same every month). Next, I added as many of our variable expenses as I could think of. Things like groceries, gas, and certain utilities where the amount can differ from month to month. For those, I filled in what I estimated we would spend. With any money that was left over, Sam and I knew the drill: It was going straight to whatever debt we were paying off at the moment.

But as noble as this budget was, one of the problems with paper is that it stays where you left it. And you probably don't have each budget category memorized, or a detail of what you've spent thus far. Therefore, if you want any sort of accuracy about what you're spending, you are constantly doing the old-school "balance the checkbook" routine.

Sam and I literally had a ledger in which we would write down each purchase. Then I kept running totals for each individual category so we would know what was left. This was painstaking, exhausting, and not nearly accurate enough on a day-to-day basis. Not to mention that in our case, there were two of us, which meant our communication had to be on point. Otherwise, if someone didn't write down their purchase right after the fact, or at least tell the other person what they spent, pandemonium could easily ensue.

I'm not gonna lie. In those early days, we overdrew a lot. Not for lack of discipline, but for lack of efficiency and our individual learning curves. BUT it did teach me diligence with money. I learned the habit of checking our accounts daily to see what had cleared and to be sure no funny business was going on.

Paper makes it hard for each person to be in the know in real time. And I can tell you there is always one nerd who likes the paper budget done just so, and they find it irritating when the other spouse doesn't do it that way. Okay, LOL, was it just me? Maybe I'm the drama. But some of y'all know what I'm talking about!

The other problem with paper—well, maybe not so much of a problem, more like an inconvenience—is the fact that each month you have to write everything out all over again. Even if you get clever and download one of those cute little budget worksheets from Etsy (which they didn't have in my day), you still need to personalize it each month by writing in your categories and estimating your dollar amounts again. It's not hard, but it's a headache and it's time-consuming. Not to mention that if you use paper, it involves math. Sure, it's the easy kind: addition and subtraction. But if you want to be accurate, you must do it down to the penny, no rounding up or down. Which means you have to check your work a couple of times to be sure you didn't flub. Because if you flub, it could mean the difference of $1, $10, or $100, depending on where you accidentally put that decimal. (Can you tell you're hearing from someone who has done this? Far more times than I'm willing to admit!)

Look, I'm just saying that doing a budget on paper is an acceptable way to budget, but it's certainly not the best way. It's not hard per se; it's just a headache, and it's time-consuming, and it requires a ton of coordination if you're doing it with a spouse.

The Issue with Spreadsheets

Then you've got the next installment in the evolution of budgeting: the spreadsheet.

Here's my argument. I HATE spreadsheets.

There, I said it. They involve formulas and math and all the nerdy number things I can't stand.

I gave spreadsheets the old college try, and I wasn't a fan. So if I must have a spreadsheet to do a budget, I'm peacing out. For me, spreadsheets are right up there with watching paint dry . . . not fascinating. Not to mention, yet again, that they don't travel with you and there is always one spouse who's a little left out in the cold (and in this case, it's probably because they want to be).

I won't belabor this subject. I'll just end with saying that spreadsheets are probably better than paper budgets, but in my educated and time-tested opinion, spreadsheets are also not the best way to budget.

The Best Way to Budget

In 2017, a tool came on the personal finance scene that changed everything. It was called EveryDollar. It was a budgeting app created by Ramsey Solutions, Dave Ramsey's company, and it totally changed the game for Sam and me.

Gone were the days of sheets and sheets of paper. No more calculators. No more spreadsheets. No more arguments about who forgot to write down their purchase in the ledger. Instead, we could set up our standard budget in the EveryDollar app and, *voila*, we both had it on our mobile phones. Which meant I could easily open the app at the grocery store to see how much was left to spend. I could quickly find out if Sam had made the rent payment or whether we had a life insurance premium due this month. Not to mention that from our own devices (not one jankety checkbook ledger), we could add transactions to any budget category and it would do the math automatically. Or if we so chose, we could connect EveryDollar to our bank to make it even easier. Our transactions would show up automatically for us to drag to the proper category, and the app would automatically update with the new amount available to spend. GAMEchanger.

EveryDollar has only improved year over year. More recently, our app developers added a feature that solves for one of the greatest stumbling blocks to budgeting: the irregular income. *Irregular income* is where a person doesn't make the same amount per month and also, in many cases, doesn't get paid on the same days every month.

Sam and I have had irregular incomes our entire career, and I would be lying if I said this wasn't a severe pain point. We knew we would likely earn enough money each month to cover our bills and debt-payoff goals, but the issue was always planning WHEN we could make our payments. It was a delicate balancing act. If you spent too much too soon, or paid the wrong bills first, you risked running out of money and having a totally broke week, or worse, being late on a bill or even accidentally overdrawing the bank account. It took constant care and attention to detail, and even still, we sometimes came up short.

EveryDollar totally solved that problem. The added feature, called "paycheck planning," helps you decide—based on your income and expenses—the right days to make each payment so that you can successfully cashflow the entire month without incident. It literally takes you one-by-one through your expenses, and you can tell Every-Dollar what date you want to pay it. If there's a problem, the app will do the math for you and either green-light it or red-light it. I tell you,

I broke out into a full-fledged praise dance when this feature rolled out! Yet again, EveryDollar completely changed the game for our budgeting routine.

Hey, some of y'all nerd out on spreadsheets; I nerd out on EveryDollar.

It just works. And to make matters even better, a year or so ago, EveryDollar rolled out another great feature: the financial roadmap tool. With this, you can plan for your future. You plug in numbers and look ahead to see, for example, how fast your student loans would be knocked out if you paid extra. Or how much you would retire with if you set aside a certain amount out of every paycheck. Or how quickly you could save up an emergency fund. It's absolutely incredible! Trust and believe me when I tell you that NOTHING will clear out toxic BS like seeing the true numbers in living color right in front of you! You can't argue with math, especially when EveryDollar is doing the math for you.

Long before I even started working for Ramsey Solutions, I quickly realized EveryDollar was *THE ONLY* solution for my budgeting needs. And I've been excited to share that solution with anyone else who will listen.

Over the years I've had the great privilege of sitting down with folks in my community, close friends, and family, helping them create an EveryDollar budget for the first time. Seeing them get started is a joy, but the VERY best part has been following their budgeting journey and getting to watch what happens after a couple of years or, sometimes, even within a few short months. What happens is, my phone starts to light up—phone call after phone call, text message after text message.

"Hey, I wanted to tell you, WE'RE DEBT-FREE!!! Over 90K paid off!"

"I wanted to thank you and Sam . . . our marriage is better than ever."

"Jade, I paid off my student loans!!"

"I've never felt so free! Girl, we actually have SAVINGS!"

"Guess what?!?! We paid off our HOUSE!!!!"

What I'm telling you is, EveryDollar is the best tool. First of all, it's free. Second of all, it helps free up both of your hands so you can finally use the budgeting tool effectively and with precision. If you do nothin' else after reading this book, download the EveryDollar app. Did I mention it's TOTALLY FREE?

Download it and you will see for your-self what I'm talking about. This is not your dad's budget; this is not your ex-husband's or ex-wife's budget; this is not that toxic sheet of paper or spreadsheet you grew up with. *This* one is all YOURS! You get to craft it, you get

Scan to start budgeting.

to tell it what to do, you get to decide. EveryDollar's job is simply to make it easier and guide you whenever you get hung up. It's full of teaching and suggestions to make sure you are winning in whatever ways you want to win.

This budget is not a punishment. This budget is your path to peace with your money . . . finally.

Sweet Freedom

"I think we're gonna need two carts," I tell my husband. It's Saturday, and Costco is slammed. We will spend the next hour fighting the crowded aisles and filling up our carts with everything I have written down (and a few extras that weren't on the list). "*Ooooo*, glass Tupperware! I could use that. I keep losing mine at work."

I put it in my cart. I don't blink, and my husband doesn't flinch.

Our family moved to Middle Tennessee a year ago. We live just south of Nashville, and there is no Costco near our house, so we have to drive 25 minutes up the highway to get to one. I don't do all my shopping at Costco, but once a month we head into the craziness to stock up. Our kids are at the age of snacking nonstop, and those Costco-sized containers of trail mix, fruit bars, and the like are the only things that seem to last through the week.

Just as I suspected, that second cart comes in handy for holding the massive package of bathroom tissue, but I also grab an 18-pack of paper towels and one of those giant supplies of Kleenex tissue. Because I can.

We get to the checkout, and like clockwork, my husband looks at me and gives his best prediction of what the bill will be. I smile, give a rebuttal on why his number is way off, and declare my much-more-accurate estimate.

As the cashier begins ringing up our items, my stomach involuntarily starts to twist into a familiar knot. I then quickly do my mental work and remind myself, *Jade, you're not broke anymore. The money is in the account. You are responsible with your money. This is in the budget. Life is good.*

I look at the little display to see the final amount. $673.29. Of course Sam's estimate was close. And I was waaaaay off. He almost always wins.

I hand the cashier my debit card without hesitation.

Approved.

Oh, thank you, Lord! I exhale. I smile at the cashier. "Thanks! Have a great weekend!"

My husband and I push the two heavy carts to where our Yukon is parked. It's a used model we bought with cash just a few months ago. After sacrificing for over a decade to pay off our debt, build up our savings, and purchase our home, this is the first time in 13 years that we are a two-car family again.

I put the kids in their car seats and help Sam load our groceries into the trunk. I take my seat on the passenger side. I relax my head back, close my eyes, and exhale a sigh of gratefulness.

I'm fine, we're fine, everything is fine. Everything is fine and dandy and okay.

And this time, it's true.

Did this book positively impact your life?

If so, it would be a huge help to me if you post about it on social media using #theramseyway. This is how we get the word out to help more people.